50

BOYFRIENDS

WORSE
THAN
YOURS

50

BOYFRIENDS

WORSE THAN YOURS

Justin Racz

BLOOMSBURY

Published by Bloomsbury Publishing, New York and London
Distributed to the trade by Holtzbrinck Publishers

All papers used by Bloomsbury Publishing are natural, recyclable products made from
wood grown in well-managed forests. The manufacturing processes conform to the
environmental regulations of the country of origin.

Library of Congress Cataloging-in-Publication Data has been applied for.

ISBN 1-59691-056-9
ISBN-13 978-1-59691-056-0

First U.S. Edition 2006

1 3 5 7 9 10 8 6 4 2

Designed by Justin Racz and Elizabeth Van Itallie
Printed in Singapore by Tien Wah Press

To Julie, my girlfriend,
Betsy Lerner, my superagent,
and Mom—
the women in my life.

Contents

1. Boyfriendster

2. Goth Casual

3. Large-Pet Owner

4. BFN (Boyfriend for Now)

5. Stalker

6. Worst Kisser Ever

7. Thrifty

8. Better Looking Than You

9. One-Position Peter

10. Friendly Neighborhood Pot Dealer

11. Home Video Maker

12. Wiener Mobile Driver

13. Grew Up Gotti

14. In the Closet

15. Grandmaster

16. Mr. Anger Management

17. White Boyee

18. Doesn't Like You Like You

19. Losing His Hair and Sensitive About It

20. Man with Cats

21. Tortured Artist

22. Roommate Turned Boyfriend

23. Backhanded Complimenter

24. Fixer-Upper

25. OCD
26. Vegan
27. Personal Trainer
28. Jewish Momma's Boy
29. Surprise Sadist
30. Comedian
31. 50K Car, 30K Job
32. Jesus Beard
33. PDA Guy
34. Your Boss
35. Not Over His Ex
36. DJ
37. Mr. Miami Beach
38. Man with Beautiful Hair
39. *Star Wars* Lover
40. Neo-Patriot
41. Sexual Grinch
42. Actor/Musician/Applebee's Waiter
43. Under House Arrest
44. Activist
45. 1.5"
46. Sensitive Tattoo Man
47. Heterosexual Flight Attendant
48. Lonely Literature Reader
49. Hypochondriac Hal
50. Lactose Intolerant
51. Your Boyfriend

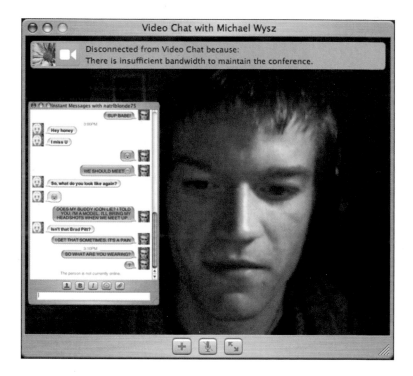

1. Boyfriendster

PROFILE

He looks great on screen at low resolution, but in person . . .

QUOTE

Hi! :)

THE DATE

Relationships begin with a month-long e-courtship built on off-the-cuff IM's at work (showing one's funny side) and witty e-mails at night. You imagine what it would be like changing your last name to Wyszomierski.

HIS PLACE

From his web cam, it looks suspiciously like a dorm room.

BENEFITS

At $29.95 a month for match.com, $34.95 for JDate, and $49.95 for eHarmony, the boy—a subscriber to all—has disposable income to burn.

DRAWBACKS

Always has e-girlfriends going on the back burner. Did your second date end at 9:30 P.M.? It's likely he's got another at 10 P.M.

2. Goth Casual

PROFILE

Not hardcore, but goth light. No fang implants or capes. Just nail polish, army boots, and a closet full of black.

THE LOOK

Black on black.

RINGTONE

A Bach funeral dirge.

HIS PLACE

Gargoyles and purple velvet spruce up his studio apartment.

BENEFITS

You can share his makeup. And it's not the cheap stuff; we're talking MAC, Laura Mercier, and Kiehl's.

DRAWBACKS

This is where he truly bares his dark side. Expect bondage, role-playing, candelabras, and crucifixes.

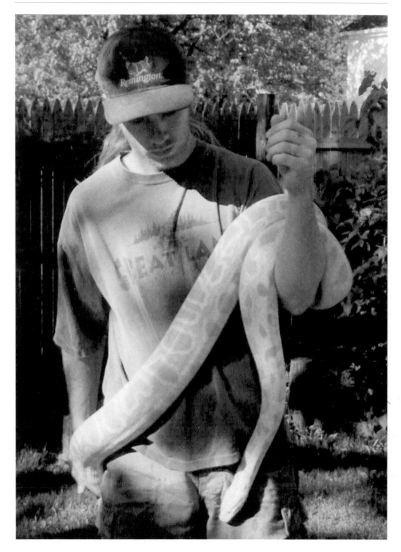

3. Large-Pet Owner

PROFILE

Whether he cares for a cobra, Egyptian King lizard, or Bengal tiger, the large-pet owner silently begs for companionship, to be held, to be loved by another. Yet like his pets, he is not the most intimate of creatures. Venomous or not, they are his guards against rejection and getting too close.

THE LOOK

He wears his boa like a boa.

QUOTE

"Pet my python?"

HIS PLACE

Temperature-controlled, habitat-friendly, smells like a zoo.

BENEFITS

His favorite DVD is *Barnyard Action Girls III: Into the Wild.* That's good if you liked *Barnyard Action Girls II: Into Eden.*

DRAWBACKS

There's no room in a relationship for a girlfriend and a python. Sooner or later one of you must go. And it's hard to kick out a snake.

4. BFN (Boyfriend for Now)

PROFILE

He's okay. Nothing special.

THE LOOK

Jeans, pocket T, L.L. Bean plaid shirt—or nothing.

RINGTONE

Stephen Stills's "If you can't be with the one you love, love the one you're with."

THE DATE

Meet up at a singles bar so you can keep your eye out for someone better.

BENEFITS

Someone to bring to family weddings so your aunt won't keep insinuating you're a lesbian.

DRAWBACKS

BFN can turn into HFN (Hubby for Now) and you end up on the wrong side of the 50/50 divorce rate statistic.

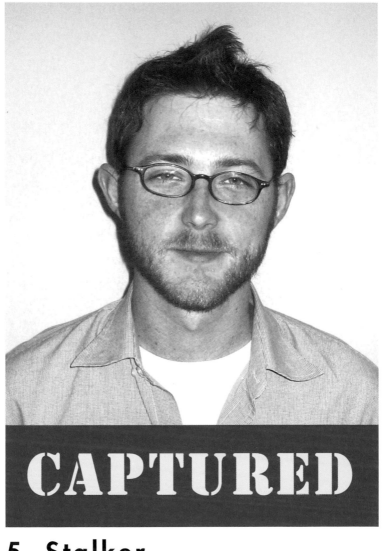

CAPTURED

5. Stalker

PROFILE

You don't ever have to worry about this guy not returning your calls or standing you up. He always remembers to call. Every ten minutes. From the street across from your apartment. Where he can see you.

THE DATE

On your first date, he stares at you for a few beats too long. He already knows everything about you: your favorite shoe store, where you get your coffee, how you like it, and the name of the barista behind the counter that you smiled at so sweetly.

RINGTONE

The Police's "Every Breath You Take."

HIS PLACE

Freshly wallpapered with a mural-size photo of you, covering up 5x7's of last year's lucky girl.

BENEFITS

If you want an attentive boyfriend, he's your man.

DRAWBACKS

If you want a restraining order, he's your man.

6. Worst Kisser Ever

PROFILE

He's perfect. Until he opens his mouth.

THE LOOK

Always has lip balm on hand.

QUOTE

"*Again*? Are you sure? It doesn't *look* like you have a cold sore."

THE DATE

He drives you up to make-out point—and locks the doors.

BENEFITS

Only you know his dirty secret.

DRAWBACKS

Nobody likes a tongue bath.

7. Thrifty

PROFILE

Chuck E. Cheese on the first date? That should have been a red flag. And when you do go out to a place without skeeball, he doesn't order dessert. He'll just have a bite of yours. And when the check comes he'll slip in a two-for-one entrée coupon.*

THE LOOK

Last year's Old Navy khakis and denim shirt off the clearance rack.

RINGTONE

Whatever came with the phone. And don't expect many calls if you're not in his friends and family network. Minutes aren't cheap.

HIS PLACE

You'll be spending nights at his one-room studio having pasta à la olive oil dinners, apple and honey for dessert, and network TV. Cable isn't cheap.

BENEFITS

The best things in life are free.

DRAWBACKS

He's in it for the long haul. Not with you, with his money. What he saves (not) spending on you, he's socking away in a tax-free Roth IRA.

*Of equal or lesser value.

8. Better Looking Than You

PROFILE

He gets stares from both sexes. It does not feel good to have guys come up to you, assuming you're just a friend, and ask if he's single.

THE LOOK

Perfect skin, the bastard. Not one whitehead or black-head.

OCCUPATION

Actor. Had a recurring role on *The Guiding Light*.

HIS RIDE

A convertible, of course.

BENEFITS

You are the envy of all your friends.

DRAWBACKS

Your "friends" have no problem propositioning him while you're in the bathroom.

9. One-Position Peter

PROFILE

Never strays from missionary.

QUOTE

"When something works for me, I stick with it."

OCCUPATION

High school history teacher. Nice fixed schedule.

BEDROOM

Give the female the bird's-eye view? It just doesn't work for him. When pushed, he says it has something to do with an old fencing injury.

BENEFITS

At least he's not in the closet.

DRAWBACKS

He's also the One-Minute Man.

10. Friendly Neighborhood Pot Dealer

PROFILE

It seems he never has time for you. He can't even talk on the phone. He says the feds are closing in and have tapped his lines, maybe yours, too. If you really want to talk, drive to a phone booth and use a land line.

THE LOOK

Sometimes he looks at you suspiciously, like you're a narc about to turn him in. If he doesn't start giving you some QT you just might.

RINGTONE

Cypress Hill's "Hits from the Bong."

HIS RIDE

Your car—in which he keeps a stash taped inside the tire hub.

BENEFITS

He does pro bono, offering a Deals-On-Wheels service for the elderly who have painful arthritis and advanced rheumatism.

DRAWBACKS

He never invites you back to his place. You might be a screamer, and if a neighbor calls in a domestic disturbance, the cops could break down his door and find his supply. And that's his third strike.

11. Home Video Maker

PROFILE

This "documentarian" would love to cast you in his third "film," the final installment in his tryptic: The first was called *Jenny*. The second, *Courtney*.

QUOTE

"It's an art house film, baby."

INCOME

He's banking on you getting famous like Paris Hilton did after her home video, so he can sell his over the Internet.

BEDROOM

A lot of direction. "Good, now turn left . . ."

BENEFITS

Hopefully you'll get your own show, just like Paris.

DRAWBACKS

Well, at least you can sue him if it hits.

12. Wiener Mobile Driver

PROFILE

He travels a lot for work. And it's hard to maintain a long distance relationship when you know he's spending every waking hour with a female co-worker inside a twenty-seven-foot motorized phallus.

RINGTONE

Something by Snoop Dogg.

HIS PLACE

A hot dog.

HIS RIDE

A hot dog.

BENEFITS

Free lunch and dinner when you're on the road with him.

DRAWBACKS

A wanderlust and a wienerlust, his love for pork, chicken, beef, and pork by-product overpowers his love for you.

13. Grew Up Gotti

PROFILE

He claims he's half Gotti, half Jewish. But it's the Sicilian that comes out, mostly out of his undershirt.

THE LOOK

Don't touch the hair, ever. Or the visor and baseball hat on backwards or cocked to the side.

READS

N/A

HIS PLACE

His parents' house. It's gaudy and gold leafed: the mirror, the dining room table, the chairs, the menorah.

BENEFITS

He always has a roll of cash that he peels from in public.

DRAWBACKS

It's mostly ones.

14. In the Closet

PROFILE

He masquerades under the auspices of being a metro-sexual. If the falsetto laugh doesn't tip you off, maybe the box set of *Queer as Folk* will give you a clue.

THE LOOK

Not to stereotype, but wearing white after Labor Day is a dead giveaway.

HIS RIDE

Likes to travel to NYC when it just so happens to be Fleet Week. The sailors parade the sidewalks in their caps, trim uniforms, and pressed and tapered pants. Adorable!

BEDROOM

N/A

BENEFITS

He's kind, gentle, and *loves* Alvin Ailey.

DRAWBACKS

What's up with all those phone calls on his cell phone bill from a guy named Maurice?

15. Grandmaster

PROFILE

Like his opponents, he's three steps ahead of your game. He never lets his guard down and always makes the first move.

RINGTONE

Wagner's "Ride of the Valkyries."

READS

Chess Life magazine.

HIS RIDE

An old Mazda with the bumper sticker "I'd Rather Be Mating."

BENEFITS

When the grandmaster is on tour he takes you with him. And the minibar is always on the house.

DRAWBACKS

After sex he says, "Checkmate."

16. Mr. Anger Management

PROFILE

After punching a maître d' three months ago, he's finally graduated from a court-appointed anger management course.

THE LOOK

A crisp business suit and a twitching jaw muscle.

RINGTONE

Currently doesn't have a cell phone—he broke his last one when his minutes ran out.

HIS PLACE

The living room features a punching bag with his boss's face on it.

BENEFITS

His incredibly aggressive manner can get you great service.

DRAWBACKS

His incredibly aggressive manner can get him thrown in jail.

17. White Boyee

PROFILE

He has mad skillz and doesn't front. He protects his woman by throwing wild gang signs Edward Scissorhands-style.

THE LOOK

Our man takes care of his appearance. Expect a satin sweat suit and bling. For a chapeau he tops it off with a bandana, sheer do-rag, or phat visor worn at a strict 30-degree angle—sometimes all three at the same time.

RINGTONE

P. Diddy, Vanilla Ice retro beat. Eminem.

HIS RIDE

A "sweet" BMX bike.

BENEFITS

He always has your back. Not when paying the meal, though.

DRAWBACKS

Virgin.

18. Doesn't Like You Like You

PROFILE

Ikey is so cute and nice and you have play dates which are fun. But is there something more going on? He puts out all these mixed signals. No fair!

THE LOOK

OshKosh B'Gosh.

THE DATE

You're not the only one he has play dates with.

HIS RIDE

Razor scooter.

BENEFITS

For Valentine's Day he made you a heart Valentine's Day card and signed it "Like, Ikey."

DRAWBACKS

He also gave one to Lori and signed it "LOVE, Ikey."

19. Losing His Hair and Sensitive About It

PROFILE

Odds are your man does not look like Bruce Willis or Ving Rhames. Think baseball caps and latent depression.

THE LOOK

Goatee: a must-have. It redirects attention to where there's hair from where there's not.

QUOTE

"Does this shampoo have minoxidil in it?"

OCCUPATION

He's heavily invested in a small pharmaceutical company that claims to have the cure for baldness, the plague of the twenty-first century—well, at least it is in *his* world.

BENEFITS

If he ever mentions your extra pounds, you can just look north of his eyes. That will keep him in check.

DRAWBACKS

His hairline is directly linked to his mojo. The follicularly challenged are wounded lions, and the thorn can never be removed.

20. Man with Cats

PROFILE

Independent, regal, superior, jealous—not him, his cats, Shelby, Kiki, and Cassandra. He's the opposite: submissive, shy, and lonely. He lets them run his life. Now that you're in the picture, you have to compete with his girls, who do *not* like another woman in the house.

RINGTONE

Song from the Meow Mix commercial: "Meow, meow, meow, meow. Meow, meow, meow, meow."

HIS PLACE

Small, dimly lit, with hair-covered furniture. And the Fresh Step ain't smelling so fresh.

HIS RIDE

Enjoy romantic getaways in his Toyota hatchback, just the five of you.

BENEFITS

Could be worse. He could be a bird man who doesn't believe in keeping them caged.

DRAWBACKS

Three sets of claws, all aimed at you. It hasn't been this bad since junior high.

21. Tortured Artist

PROFILE

He's very sweet and thoughtful when the numerous inner demons and voices in his head subside. His constant creativity extends into the bedroom, where he will use found art and paintbrushes as tools of seduction.

THE LOOK

Always sporting a smock or overalls, usually splattered with blood, sweat, tears, paint, and plaster. The amount of blood should never exceed that of the other substances. If it does, you might accidentally be dating a serial killer instead.

QUOTE

"Okay, turn your chin slightly toward me. A little less. Perfect. Now hold that for an hour and a half."

HIS PLACE

His studio/home/storage facility is cluttered with mannequins, dolls, paint, love letters, mason jars filled with his own tears, and unpaid bills.

BENEFITS

He is a generous gift giver during courtship.

DRAWBACKS

Gifts consist of Popsicle sticks glued together and little fat-woman wire figurines.

22. Roommate Turned Boyfriend

PROFILE

Is it love or is it convenience? He says he loves you but he also says it's your turn to clean the bathroom.

QUOTE

"You want to order in Chinese?"

THE DATE

He doesn't have to take you out to get you back to his place.

HIS PLACE

It's his name on the lease, so he always has hand.

BENEFITS

You'll never get a booty call. Just a booty knock.

DRAWBACKS

When you need some space from him, there's nowhere to go. Even Chandler and Monica had a hallway between them.

23. Backhanded Complimenter

PROFILE

He's the author of such gems as "You look so beautiful with makeup on" and "Those jeans are nice and slimming."

THE DATE

"Wow, you look a lot better than your picture!"

2ND DATE

"You can take the bread away. She ate pasta for lunch."

3RD DATE

"Oh, do you keep your hair up mostly? I liked the way your bangs fell in front of your face last time."

BENEFITS

Likes to buy you gifts. Like spa certificates and expensive acne-fighting facial products.

DRAWBACKS

Years of therapy once you break up with him.

BEFORE
YOU

AFTER
YOU

24. Fixer-Upper

PROFILE

He's perfect. That is, as soon as you get rid of his tapered jeans and white old-man sneakers . . . and get him a dermatologist and a gym membership. But where to begin?

THE LOOK

Geek. But soon: Chic.

THE DATE

In the beginning, think indoors—private, not public. When he's presentable, that's when you roll him out like a Cover Girl advertising campaign.

HIS PLACE

Looks like a holdover from the dorm days, with the requisite *Scarface* and *Godfather* posters taped to the wall. It's your job to refurnish and redecorate.

BENEFITS

Little competition. Most girls aren't looking for a project; they're looking for the finished piece. Oh, the pride you feel once his makeover's complete!

DRAWBACKS

Sprucing him up is an investment that might not yield the best return. It's pure speculation. Even if it's successful, it could backfire: he might bail with new *GQ* confidence and see what else is out there.

25. OCD

PROFILE

He's gentle, clean, and attentive. He never leaves the toilet seat up. But he will lift it and close it ten times as part of his ritual.

THE LOOK

Instead of shaking hands with people, he bows.

QUOTE

"Uh-oh. Our spoons are facing in different directions."

HIS PLACE

Meticulous. Every book and CD is alphabetically organized. The remote controls are stacked in order of size. Frankly, it's a little creepy.

BENEFITS

He made an exception for your father, and shook his hand.

DRAWBACKS

Then he immediately whipped out the antibacterial lotion in front of him.

26. Vegan

PROFILE

If you're not a vegetarian, vegan, or fruitarian, forget it. He's not interested.

QUOTE

"No whey, José!"

THE DATE

Lentil bar.

HIS PLACE

Shares a house with other food purists. Vegetable garden in the back. Prepare to hoe.

BENEFITS

He has incredible compassion for animals and is in touch with his feelings.

DRAWBACKS

When kissing, he can smell the bacon on your breath.

27. Personal Trainer

PROFILE

He is the master and you are the servant. He says bend, you say how low.

THE LOOK

Shouldn't you be the one wearing Spandex?

QUOTE

"Are you ready to sweat?"

THE DATE

All the egg white omelets you can eat.

BENEFITS

A great body. And a 25% discount on gym membership.

DRAWBACKS

Break up and you will have to switch gyms.

28. Jewish Momma's Boy

PROFILE

His name starts with a J: Josh, Jason, Jared, or Jacob. His middle name is Scott, David, or Mark.

THE LOOK

Very groomed, very gelled. Until he's twenty-five, when it starts thinning on top.

OCCUPATION

Mommy's so proud because he's an investment banker at Goldman Sachs!

HIS RIDE

He sold his car now that he's moved from Long Island and into the city.

BENEFITS

You can use his parents' house in the Hamptons.

DRAWBACKS

He will never treat you better than he treats his mother.

29. Surprise Sadist

PROFILE

You date, you introduce him to your parents, you move in. You think you know him until he takes down his fraternity paddle from the wall and says bend over.

THE LOOK

His hair is neat, his collars are crisp, his leather is tight, and his dog collar is ready.

QUOTE

"Variety is the spice of life."

OCCUPATION

Dental hygienist.

BENEFITS

If you're a masochist, you've found your mate.

DRAWBACKS

If you don't like clubbing midweek on fetish night and performing voyeuristic acts in a cage, you're in trouble.

30. Comedian

PROFILE

He wants you for material. After three years working the clubs with the same routine, he's desperate for some new jokes, and you're likely the butt of them.

THE LOOK

Big ties, bad hair, lots of hand gesturing.

THE DATE

On your first date, he dressed up as a woman. Not funny.

HIS RIDE

His horn? "La Cucaracha."

BENEFITS

You got a free cruise when he landed a summer gig on a Royal Caribbean liner.

DRAWBACKS

Your bad sex life got great laughs on Leno.

31. 50K Car, 30K Job

PROFILE

He spares no expense. Not on you, on his phatty Escalade. Twenty-inch $500 spinning chrome rims? Standard.

THE LOOK

Custom-tailored Louis Vuitton leather front seats, armrests, and steering wheel.

THE DATE

He parks, you two move to the back seat and watch a DVD in the front seat headrest.

HIS RIDE

You'll spend many a date riding shotgun, cruising at a comfortable 15 mph so he can check out who's checking his ride out.

BENEFITS

He lives for today. 60K in debt, the last thing he wants to think about is tomorrow. It's not the destination, it's the journey. Enjoy the pimped ride.

DRAWBACKS

No beverages in the car. Corinthian leather stains easily.

32. Jesus Beard

PROFILE

He has a slight God complex. He thinks having the beard of the Messiah makes him holier than thou, but it just makes it difficult to get a good table at a restaurant. The freaks always get seated in the back.

THE LOOK

Technically, it's divine. But really it's just shaggy and unkempt (and not so great-smelling, either).

RINGTONE

Something by Phish.

HIS RIDE

Mom's old Volvo.

BENEFITS

When he realizes corporate America requires a clean shave, that crumb-catcher will come right off.

DRAWBACKS

When it does, it will reveal a weak chin and bad skin.

33. PDA Guy

PROFILE

It's one thing to be affectionate with a lover in public; it's another to hike you up on the restaurant table.

THE LOOK

Cheshire cat smile, like he's up to no good and can pounce at any time.

RINGTONE

The Beatles' "Why Don't We Do It in the Road?"

HIS RIDE

A suspicious fondness for public transportation.

BENEFITS

You'll certainly feel loved.

DRAWBACKS

Public indecency can get you two to four in most states.

34. Your Boss

PROFILE

Ten years in middle management and he's still not going anywhere. So at least he can fish off the company pier.

QUOTE

"You're first in line for a promotion. Meet you at the hotel after work?"

RINGTONE

BTO's "Taking Care of Business."

HIS RIDE

He carpools it.

BENEFITS

He's the best-looking middle manager in the office.

DRAWBACKS

The ring is for show.

35. Not Over His Ex

PROFILE

He's with you, but his heart is still back in college where he met Laura. He says he's over her, but that's just because she's engaged now, and admitting that he still loved her would be to admit he was a fool to have ever let her go to the DKE semiformal with Chad.

 THE LOOK

When he's looking at you, you can see the sadness, the disappointment that you don't inspire him to write poetry, to cry openly—the way Laura did.

 RINGTONE

Joe Jackson's "Is She Really Going Out with Him?"

 HIS RIDE

'94 Honda Accord—the car "they" bought together.

 BENEFITS

He's trying very, very hard to fall in love with you.

 DRAWBACKS

The never-ending Laura anecdotes, punctuated by the unconvincing, "But all that's in the past."

36. DJ

PROFILE

What Jackie Robinson did for the black athlete, Fatboy Slim did for the white DJ. But now any white boy with two turntables and a microphone can say he's got rhythm. *Behind* the dance floor, that is.

THE LOOK

$160 Diesel jeans, Diesel cologne, Degree 24-hour antiperspirant. Holds headphone to his ear, head cocked like he's about to eat a taco.

THE DATE

10 P.M. to 4 A.M. at the club, Fridays and Saturdays. Standing room only.

RINGTONE

The Sugar Hill Gang's "Rapper's Delight"

BENEFITS

You get comped at the door.

DRAWBACKS

His career will crash in two years, and he'll end up doing bar mitzvahs.

37. Mr. Miami Beach

PROFILE

At seventy-five years "young," he's considered the playboy of Shady Acres Resort & Retirement.

THE LOOK

Bermuda shorts. Golf shirt. Hawaiian Tropic, SPF 4.

QUOTE

"Baby, come on, don't believe everything you hear. You're the only one."

HIS RIDE

Drive? With his glaucoma?

BENEFITS

He's the only one in the gated community who doesn't have a pacemaker.

DRAWBACKS

You saw him speaking with Crystal at the pool. And she has the big condo on the golf course. How can you compete with Crystal? She's got the boobs of a woman half her age—which would be thirty-five.

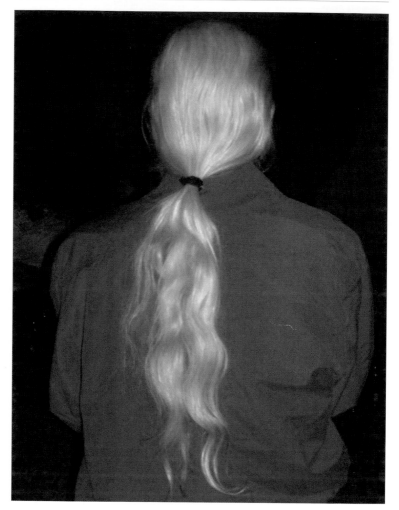

38. Man With Beautiful Hair

PROFILE

Sometimes it feels like you're dating his hair. It's gorgeous, blond, flowing, luxurious hair—undeniably better than yours.

THE LOOK

Full-bodied and fabulous. Unfortunately, it takes him half an hour to blow dry. You compete with him for mirror time.

QUOTE

"It's a gift, sure, but it's hard work too."

BEDROOM

Looking up at him, it's like you're humping a thoroughbred.

BENEFITS

No Rogaine for this man.

DRAWBACKS

With all the hair product spilling over from the bathroom and into the house, you wonder if there's room in the relationship for you.

39. *Star Wars* Lover

PROFILE

If Yoda was around, he'd slap this kid upside the head and tell him to log off of Starwarsrumors.com and take you out to a nice dinner.

THE DATE

A weekend in beautiful, sunny California—entirely spent indoors, at a sci-fi convention.

HIS RIDE

Toyota Corolla, a.k.a. the *Millennium Falcon*.

BEDROOM

You dress up as Queen Amidala, he slips into his wookiee mask.

BENEFITS

Since you're the only girl in his group of sci-fi geeks, you're guaranteed an intoxicating local fame.

DRAWBACKS

Thinks it's hot when he speaks to you in Klingon. Yeah, he's a Trekkie, too.

40. Neo-Patriot

PROFILE

His façade is all flag, snarl, and chewing tobacco. But underneath is a scared little boy whose mom will Greyhound his butt to Canada if Bush reinstates the draft.

THE LOOK

Part Bruce Springsteen "Born in the USA," part American Chopper, part NYC sidewalk T-shirt impulse buy.

HIS PLACE

The room he grew up in. In exchange for free post–high school lodging, he suffers the ignominy of doing chores. His tour of duty is taking out the trash, rinsing dishes, and bringing his stuff up from the bottom of the stairs.

BEDROOM

He's coined a new move called "The Fast & the Furious." Likes to hear Survivor's "Eye of the Tiger" in the background.

BENEFITS

If you like trucks and hunting, he's your man.

DRAWBACKS

His immediate plans in life are to make his car payments and have sex with you.

41. Sexual Grinch

PROFILE

Doesn't understand the meaning of the word "reciprocity."

THE LOOK

Satisfied.

OCCUPATION

Corporate lawyer.

BEDROOM

He gets a full night's sleep every night. You go to bed angry and frustrated. Why not tell him what you want and need? It would ruin what you have outside the bedroom.

BENEFITS

He's wonderful in all the other areas. He holds the door open for you; always pays for dinner; treats you to vacations; says God bless you when you sneeze. A good man like that is hard to find.

DRAWBACKS

Sometimes you see yourself married, three kids, driving a Mercedes SUV, with his and hers affairs on the side.

42. Actor / Musician / Applebee's Waiter

PROFILE

Still waiting for his big break, he's working nights at the 'bees, so he can audition during the day. So far his parts have included Murder Victim on *Law & Order*, Cow for the National Dairy Board convention, and Frozen Drink Guy at the Comic Strip. He also sings and plays the guitar, but not very well.

THE LOOK

Keeps nails long for fingerpicking; $100 haircut so he'll be ready when an agent calls.

RINGTONE

"42nd Street."

BEDROOM

Here he likes to show off his range of foreign accents.

BENEFITS

Free scoop of ice cream with your order of pie.

DRAWBACKS

He's not even a good waiter. And he spends all his extra money on teeth-whitening strips.

43. Under House Arrest

PROFILE

Though he still claims his innocence, he is electronically leashed to his house for the next year. He's now running an illegal online poker ring.

THE LOOK

Bathrobe.

QUOTE

"There's nothing to see in the theaters. And you can't even get authentic red sauce in restaurants anyways."

THE DATE

For your anniversary, he went beyond his restricted radius and past his 6 P.M. curfew.

BENEFITS

After six months sitting at home watching the Food Channel, he's become quite the chef.

DRAWBACKS

He has a lot of time to plot his revenge for those who ratted him out.

44. Activist

PROFILE

He's passionate and driven about causes—Save the Humpbacks, free Tibet, Give a Hoot, Don't Pollute. Your importance ranks somewhere between landfill dumping and stem cell research. This relationship will not work if you're from a red state.

THE LOOK

No logos.

THE DATE

He invites you to picket a recently reviewed restaurant because he found out the chef doesn't use free-range chicken and makes his dishwashers work unseemly hours for little pay.

READS

The Nation.

BENEFITS

He's also passionate and driven in bed.

DRAWBACKS

He'd rather be chained to the White House gate for two days than go to Cape Cod for the weekend.

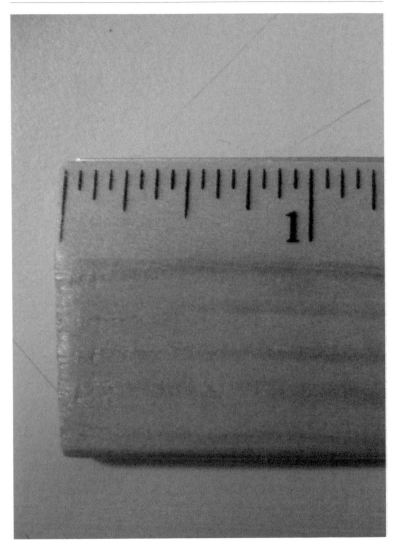

45. 1.5"

PROFILE

He's tried all the creams, all the machinery. He buys into the late night commercials promising growth. But until there's a cure, he must be the most creative person in the bedroom, ever.

THE LOOK

Attractive, athletic, stylish haircut. And yet . . .

QUOTE

"It's not the size of the wave but the motion of the ocean." (Pond is more like it.)

BEDROOM

A hyper-enthusiastic combination of acrobatics, Tantric research, and selflessness—all tinged, however, with shame.

BENEFITS

Roses, jewelry, vacations—he will do anything to make you stay. After all, he's dating Mother Teresa.

DRAWBACKS

Eventually, you'll get tired of the Art of the Sensual Massage. It just doesn't compare to the horizontal hustle. And this guy can't dance.

46. Sensitive Tattoo Man

PROFILE

You think you're getting a Harley-Davidson, but you end up with a Schwinn.

THE LOOK

The giant spread-eagle tattoo spanning his chest is actually a prank his fraternity brothers played on him.

HIS PLACE

French drapes and 420-count Egyptian cotton sheets.

HIS RIDE

The low rider chopper in the garage? His brother's. The Cabriolet? His.

BENEFITS

He's not afraid to cry . . .

DRAWBACKS

. . . while watching Lifetime.

47. Heterosexual Flight Attendant

PROFILE

A rooster in the henhouse.

THE LOOK

Uncomfortable dark blue or burgundy wool suit that desperately tries to look official.

HIS PLACE

Only there half the time. The other half he's commingling with his co-workers at the airport Marriott.

HIS RIDE

No car. He takes the train to the plane.

BENEFITS

Free trips, but not on blackout dates.

DRAWBACKS

Flight attendant ranks just below male nurse in the macho category.

48. Lonely Literature Reader

PROFILE

He's so busy trying to find himself, he has little time for you. Always in a funk, he blames society, phonies, and materialism . . . but then why is he hanging out at the mall?

THE LOOK

Black, grays, $300 Armani reading glasses.

THE DATE

Two hours spent milling around dusty used-book store aisles.

READS

Dostoevsky, Tolstoy, Kafka, Raymond Carver, *Batman* (in secret)

BENEFITS

He is very open with his emotions.

DRAWBACKS

Standing, naked, he recites his poetry to you, which sucks.

49. Hypochondriac Hal

With an encyclopedic knowledge of medical disorders and their symptoms, he can find fatality in even the most innocuous cough.

Nervously bitten inside lip, furrowed brow, palms rubbed raw from over-washing.

"I think I'm getting a sore throat."

In his closet—gas mask and old Y2K survival kit.

He knows the best medical specialists in the area.

He refuses to kiss you if you don't brush your teeth and rinse with mouthwash first.

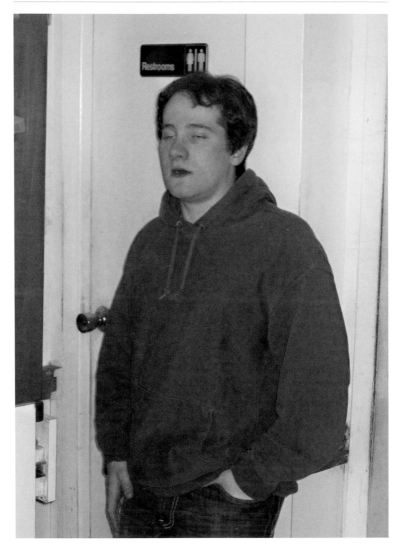

50. Lactose Intolerant

PROFILE

He actually tolerates it, enduring cramps, gas, and diarrhea for the simple pleasures in life: coffee with half and half; hot fudge sundaes. The question is, can you tolerate it?

THE LOOK

Uncomfortable and in distress.

QUOTE

"Do you have any Lactaid in your purse?"

THE DATE

You're pretty much dating his small intestine.

RINGTONE

Kelis's "Milkshake."

DRAWBACKS

If he invites you back to his place, he'd better have an air purifier.

51. Your Boyfriend

PROFILE

THE LOOK

THE DATE

RINGTONE

BENEFITS

DRAWBACKS

THE BOYFRIENDS

Boyfriendster: Michael Wyszomierski
Goth Casual: Nate Taylor
Large Pet Owner: Chris Jones; Burmese Boa, Natasha
BFN (Boyfriend For Now): Ed McGowan
Stalker: Bryan Wilson
Worst Kisser Ever: Rob Seitelman, Abby Jordan
Better Looking Than You: Eric Simmons
One-Position Peter: Colin Glaum
Neighborhood Pot Dealer: lechucks.bitacoras.com
Home Video Maker: Hunter Shawn
Grew Up Gotti: Zack Hirsch
In the Closet: Jon Daniel
Grandmaster: Ian Riddoch
Mr. Anger Management: João Paglione
White Boyee: Justin Jaffe, Per B. Chilstrom, Lawrence Ezrow, William Noto
Doesn't Like You Like You: Jackie Resnik, Ikey Schultz
Losing His Hair and Sensitive About It: Joseph Tudisco
Man with Cats: Chris McMurtrey
Tortured Artist: Daniel Berman
Roommate Turned Boyfriend: Brandon Cole, Jessica Kern
Backhanded Complimenter: Simon, Kyla Lucking
Fixer-Upper: Jermel Wilson
Vegan: Andrew Ritter, Kate Mahar
Personal Trainer: Rick Sanvik bestinform.com / Gil Nunes
Jewish Momma's Boy: Mark Mark and Mrs. Schmulen
Surprise Sadist: Anonymous
Comedian: John Watson
Jesus Beard Guy: Courtesy of Flickr
Your Boss: Rick Doerr
Not Over His Ex: Lara Tal, bad boyfriend
DJ: Kev Sands
Mr. Miami Beach: Orville Warner
Man with Beautiful Hair: Rob Rite
Star Wars Lover: Sandtrooper, Karen Grenke
Neo-Patriot: Will Steacy
Sexual Grinch: Alec Brownstein, Samantha Roberts

Actor/Musician/Applebee's: Farris Sheikh
Under House Arrest: Joe Barone
Sensitive Tattoo Man: Jon Fletcher
Hypochondriac Hal: Allen Gallehugh
Lactose Intolerant: Ben Rauch

THE PHOTOGRAPHERS

BFN, One-Position Peter: Jake Jacobs
Grandmaster: Adam Raoof
White Boyee: Mikaela L. Chilstrom
Man with Cats: Debbie McMurtrey
Tortured Artist: Joe Ovbey
Sadism: Billy Warhol
DJ: George Pollard
Man with Beautiful Hair: Les
Sexual Grinch, Not Over Ex: Julie Soefer
Under House Arrest: Jill Cheris

Contributing writers: Lori Segal, Dan Moyer, Alec Brownstein

Retouching and illustration: Julie Soefer, Eric Van Skyhawk, Laurel Tyndale

ACKNOWLEDGMENTS

You wouldn't be holding this book without my editors, and intellectual superiors, Panio Gianopoulos, Colin Dickerman, and Marisa Pagano. Their championing of these projects, wit, and forgiveness of deadlines brought a book about bad jobs to life and then gave it a brother and sister. Being in print, not once, but three times—well, I still can't believe it.

Thank you to managing editor Greg Villepique for your utmost patience; publicists Yelena Gitlin and Suzie Lee for giving me attention good enough for Grisham; designers Alona Fryman, Amy King, and Elizabeth Van Itallie for having better color sense than me. And everyone else at Bloomsbury who helped to make it happen. See you all at the book party. Open bar 9–10 P.M.

ADDITIONAL THANKS TO:

Wendy Morris PR, Alec Brownstein, Alex Finkelstein, Jasyon Atienza, Maria Pappalardo, Annie Angellino, Chuck Tso, Carrie Lipper, Annie Cooper, Hope Grider, Meira Cohen, Fiona Carter, Danny Roth, Judy Riggio, Lucia Martinez, Jeff Stock, Melinda Ward, Rick Abbott, Roy Elvove, Clayton Hemmert, Victoria Lesiw, Cheryl B. Engelhardt, Crewcuts, Quiet Man, Joshua Shabtai, Seth Godin, Ryan D'Agostino, Elizabeth Morgan, Billy Noto, Andrew Ritter, Kate Mahar, Scott Mitnick, Ben Coplon, Julie Rappaport, Jason Tandon, Clint Bierman, Chad Urmston, Katie Rosin, The Apostolati, Deborah Lester, Marianna Racz, Rebekah Racz, Matthew, Craig, Hatae, Ellen Racz, Gregory Racz, Daniel Racz, Alexa Jervis, Leslie Kantor, Adam Kantor, Josh Neuman, Allen Salkin, Dana Smith, Matt O'Hara, the Soefers, Robert Racusin, Kate Marcus, Elisa Resnik, Billy Warhol, Irregular Girl, Jonathan Solari & Sam, Benjamin Sulds, Andrew Barchilon, John Hume, Watt White, George Pollard, Noah Starr, Brandon & Drew, Jesse Resnick, Leigh Polfer, Ed Lambert, Glenn, Alix Klingenberg, Tom Connor, Chris Nichols, Amy Nichols, Rachel Seitel, Dave McClure, Brain Goff, Marc Bichet, the Maplewood Boyz, Maxine Ferman, Ira Morenberg, Gil Nunes, Jim Edgar, Nathaniel Claridad, Michael McCreighton, Anna Maj Michelson, Adam Draper, Michael Weinberg, Baruch Shemtov, Wes Putt, Nick Miles, Jeannie Hajdenberg, et. al.